essentials

Business Letters
that Work

Time-saving books that teach specific skills to busy people, focusing on what really matters; the things that make a difference – the *essentials*.

Other books in the series include:

Boost Your Word Power

Expand Your Vocabulary

Preparing a Marketing Plan

Leading Teams

Making the Most of Your Time

Solving Problems

Coaching People

Hiring People

Making Great Presentations

Writing Good Reports

The Ultimate Business Plan

Writing Business E-mails

For full details please send for a free copy of the latest catalogue. See back cover for address.

Business Letters that Work

John Greenland

ESSENTIALS

Published in 2001 by
How To Books Ltd, 3 Newtec Place,
Magdalen Road, Oxford OX4 1RE, United Kingdom
Tel: (01865) 793806   Fax: (01865) 248780
email: info@howtobooks.co.uk
www.howtobooks.co.uk

British Library Cataloguing in Publication Data
A catalogue record for this book is available from
the British Library

Edited by Diana Brueton
Cover design by Shireen Nathoo Design
Produced for How To Books by Deer Park Productions
Designed and typeset by Shireen Nathoo Design
Printed and bound in Great Britain
by Bell & Bain Ltd., Glasgow

NOTE: The material contained in this book is set out in good faith for
general guidance and no liability can be accepted for loss or expense
incurred as a result of relying in particular circumstances on statements
made in the book. The laws and regulations are complex and liable to
change, and readers should check the current position with the relevant
authorities before making personal arrangements.

ESSENTIALS *is an imprint of*
How To Books

Contents

Preface

Many people at work find letter writing an unwelcome task. They are not sure where to begin or how much to say and they can be daunted by formal business language. Yet the business letter is important in putting on record the arrangements a business makes with its customers and suppliers. That record must be clear, complete and correct.

This book sets out a methodical approach to writing business letters. The text progresses from start to finish but each section of each chapter is self-contained and you may wish to dip into particular sections again.

One of the great rewards in writing business letters is that the elements that make reading easy for your reader make writing easy for you.

John Greenland MA (Oxon.)

1 Aiming Your Letter

If you don't know where you are going,
you won't know if you've arrived.

Every letter you write projects an image of you and your organisation to the outside world. How does your customer see you: cold and formal, institutional – old-fashioned, perhaps? Or does he see you as personal and helpful – genuinely interested in his needs? Don't allow a bad letter to lose goodwill; use every letter to build a worthy image for your organisation.

Start by asking the questions of aim: why, who, what, how, when and where. The answers will point you in the right direction. A clear aim tells the reader what he needs to know but also helps you as the writer, by telling you what you do not need to write.

Is this you?

I've no idea who will read my letter. • Their letter seems very formal: do I need to be that formal? • It's all very well trying to please the reader; the first person I have to please is my boss because she has to sign my letter. • I could say quite a lot but how much detail do they need? • Who is this Admin. Manager anyway?

Know why you are writing

You have opened a letter from a customer placing an order for two circular filing systems. Only yesterday you had a letter from the same customer placing an order for two circular filing systems. Yesterday's order had come from a different address but said it was "confirmation of verbal instructions". It referred to an earlier order for filing cabinets ... Confusion abounds but you must deal with the request so you pick up a pencil or approach your keyboard to draft a reply. One hour later you tear up your fourth attempt.

You may well ask: why am I writing? Should you be writing a letter? The assumption that an incoming letter will automatically produce a reply can be limiting. In this example a telephone call to the source of the two orders would be an appropriate first step. This should clarify whether you have one order or two. The answer will allow you to reply positively. You then have on record correct information rather than evidence of your confusion.

The letter provides a permanent record of transactions between organisations. That record will guide future actions and in extreme cases may appear as evidence in court where a contract has run into delay or difficulty. Your record must be clear and correct.

Ask why you are writing and you focus on what your letter is aiming to achieve:

~ payment of an overdue account

~ sale of a new range of patio furniture

~ technical information about a fax machine

~ confirmation of arrangements for a
   meeting *

Determine who your reader is

Under pressure to clear routine
correspondence you may not give much
thought to the person who will read your
letter. You may be more aware of the person
who will sign the letter and indeed, for some
writers, satisfying that initial reader is also
part of their aim.

For incoming letters seek guidance from:

~ the name and job or department title at
   the end

~ the content of the letter.

If you initiate correspondence, target your
reader accurately. A telephone call may
determine precisely who buys computers or
who deals with queries on customer
accounts. You are then able to direct your
request to the most relevant person.

Buyer and salesman have a different
outlook on a similar product. In making a

*If you don't know
why you are
writing, what
chance does your
reader have?*

technical enquiry to the buyer you will reasonably expect a competent reply; the salesman's competence may direct you to the benefits of buying the product.

Inexperienced writers are sometimes in awe of the job title to which they must reply. Consciously writing 'up' to their reader, a strained artificiality emerges. Copied for more than a century through the filing system, we still read the quaint language of some Victorian clerk, verbally tugging his forelock in deference to his more worthy reader. *

The level of your writing must be your natural way of expressing your meaning.

Establish what your reader needs

When you respond to an incoming letter, look at what it requires:

~ Is it looking for information?

~ Does it want action?

~ What do you need to do and by when?

* *Consider your reader in order to focus on the person who is right to handle your request and to help you form an apt approach – not to write up or down.*

The incoming letter may be in response to your request for information or action. The quality of the reply will indicate the completeness and clarity of your request.

Imagine that Mr and Mrs Green have asked you to quote for a garage they saw illustrated in a magazine. They may imagine the garage installed behind a gravel drive, framed with carefully selected shrubs, adorned with a security light and a purple front door. You may be thinking of the standard Mark 1 flatpack of concrete components, craned off onto their front verge. The two pictures vary greatly, as would the costs.

Telling the reader what he needs to know may involve some investigation:

~ Is there access to the site?

~ Have you prepared a base or must we?

~ Do you want us to erect the garage, or will you use a sub-contractor? *

Readers' needs may vary even within the same organisation.

Imagine you manufacture display equipment for exhibitions and you are answering an enquiry from a potential customer's Chief Buyer. Relevant issues might be:

~ dimensions and weight of equipment

~ unit price/quantity discounts

~ lead time from order to delivery

~ carriage charges, insurance, and terms of payment.

The potential customer's Public Relations Officer who plans to use the equipment may ask:

~ Will it fit into the back of the pool car?

~ Can my assistant lift it on her own?

~ What colours does it come in?

~ Does it use pins or magnets? *

A chain of relevant needs can develop from asking sensible questions about the reader.

Consider how to approach the task

Writing is transparent: it acts as a window

through which the reader may see the personality that lies behind the words. This can be a disadvantage:

~ if your attitude is offhand

~ if you consider the reader to be an interruption to your day's work

~ if secondary factors have influenced your mood.

It can of course be a great advantage. Once you are aware that your attitude shows in writing, you can use it to great effect. Do not attempt to hide your personality; let it emerge. Show that:

~ you are able to understand the reader's problems

~ you are willing to help

~ you are patient if your reader has made a mistake or has given incomplete information. *

Your purpose in promoting such an attitude will give you greater influence with your reader when you, in your turn, are looking for results.

You will need to vary your approach. If you

are writing to complain about poor service from a supplier you will expect to be firm. You are likely to specify plainly what is wrong and to point your reader towards what he should do to put it right. This may involve target dates or times for action.

If you are writing in reply to a complaint from a customer, a firm approach may appear blunt and inappropriate. You will need to be conciliatory, although you may still wish to offer the customer a diplomatic reminder of how he might have prevented the complaint from arising.

In professional firms, letters regularly extend beyond the conventional picture of three short paragraphs on an A4 page. Such letters may:

~ offer personal financial advice

~ list evidence for submission in support of legal proceedings, or

~ specify an architect's detailed requirements for progress on a contract.

In handling more extended material you will need a more complete and visible classification of the content. This will show in headings, and perhaps in sub-headings within the narrative, to give appropriate direction to your reader.

Decide where and when to write

Your letter is about to reach its destination. How do you picture its arrival?   Royal Mail driver hands it to Office Junior. Office Junior carries it on silver platter through lengthy corridors until finally he reaches your reader. Your reader sits in smiling anticipation behind a large mahogany desk, its surface shining and empty. *

* More probably your letter will be plonked down with a pile of others in an in-tray that scarcely has room to contain them.

The mail sort will make frequent use of the adjacent bin as your busy reader separates the junk from what he feels obliged to retain. Your polished sales letter will be junk to the reader who does not actually need a set of 40mm widgets just now – even at the special offer price.

If your reader is a small sub-contractor, his office is likely to be the cab of his van and the in-tray (the pile on the dashboard) is likely to receive attention along with tea and sandwiches during the morning break. This is neither the time nor the place for an over-sophisticated approach.

Timing can be critical. Your reader will not thank you if that vital piece of information he has asked for arrives on the morning he has taken an early flight to Frankfurt to discuss its implications. *

Your sales letter must arrive at the time that relates to the budget, or the buying decision, or the need for widgets. Alternatively, it must be persuasive enough to encourage the reader to put it on record in anticipation of such a time.

Writing the letter is often only part of a wide-ranging activity that relates to the aims of your organisation but it is the vital part that puts you on record. Your aim is to see that by asking the right questions you give your letter the best chance of success.

Someone, somewhere will want your widgets but only if they are on offer at the right time.

Summary Points

★ Be certain you need to write a letter.

★ Picture your reader.

★ Think about what your reader needs to know.

★ Choose a relevant approach.

★ Relate your letter to where it will arrive.

★ Time it to have greatest impact.

2 Planning and Structuring Your Letter

A mighty maze! But not without a plan.

Some letter writers see the task as an instant mind dump in which they commit randomly to paper any vaguely relevant thought. The reader is left to unravel the tangle. It is not astonishing that letters sometimes fail to get the response the originator hoped for.

The small amount of time needed to plan more complicated letters will save you more time at the writing and editing stage. More importantly it should deliver information clearly to your intended reader. *

* The burden of producing clarity must rest with the writer.

Writers sometimes struggle to word an opening sentence before they have given thought to the letter as a whole. In planning, work from the general to the particular. The detail will then fall into place rather than obstruct your progress.

Is this you?

There is so much to cover I don't know where to begin. • What if the letter is about more than one subject? • I can't just write one line. • It's all on one subject so I put it all in one paragraph. • I don't have a problem with semi-colons; I don't use them. • Should this have come first?

List the content of your letter

Use the questions of aim to determine the content of your letter. Ask yourself:

~ Who is my reader?

~ What does my reader need to know? *

* This initial selection ensures that you offer relevant information and eliminate unnecessary detail.

To confirm your ability to attend a meeting on a certain date, a single sentence may suffice. This will not test your formatting skills but will please your reader for its directness.

I once wrote to a training officer suggesting several dates for a training course he had asked me to run. The course was to cover various aspects of writing including business letters. Imagine the training officer as a former naval captain with a crisp manner and you will appreciate his memorable reply that ran to just five words:

> Dear Mr Greenland
> 3rd, 4th and 5th: splendid!
> Yours sincerely

How many writers would have turned that content into a three paragraph letter?

Of course there are times when we must handle extensive material. You will find it helpful to be methodical in approaching the task:

~ Gather relevant information.

~ Allocate the information to main sections.

~ Give each main section a heading.

With classification it is tempting to choose general or abstract headings that allow the detail to fit comfortably. You achieve a better result by choosing more selective, more concrete headings.

It can be daunting to look at a long list of topics and to feel that you don't know where to begin. By working from general to particular you retain control. Your mental process will be: " I have a lot to cover but my letter is really about X,Y and Z. Within X it will be helpful if I discuss A,B,C and D; Y will stand alone; Z will need to break down into E and F." *

Decide the sequence of delivery

It is difficult to think about the content of your letter without giving thought to the sequence in which you will deliver it. A natural order will often emerge.

When you review activity:

~ what we have done in the past

~ how we operate currently

~ what we plan for the future.

The headings that derive from this process give the reader perspective and help to prompt your writing.

When you resolve a problem:

~ what has gone wrong

~ why it went wrong

~ what we will do to put it right.

A natural order promotes a logical flow of thinking and allows the letter to end at the point you wish to reach:

~ looking ahead rather than looking back

~ solving a problem rather than raising one.

Imagine you are writing to a customer about two orders placed with you. To process one of the orders you need more information; the other order is fine and you have already handled it. By referring first in your letter to the order you have dealt with, you are then able to end the letter by prompting the reader to supply information to deal with the other one.

For more complex letters people tend to group their material well functionally but find the sequence more challenging and often repeat material. To plan your sequence:

~ Spread your headings across the top of a sheet of A4 using the landscape or horizontal plane.

~ List the points that relate to each heading in columns.

~ Consider any changes in the sequence.

~ Decide whether larger sections should break down into sub-headings or whether additional headings would be better.

It is easier to achieve the classification in outline than to rewrite large chunks of your letter. *

An outline classification can show your intended approach to a colleague or perhaps to the signatory who will ultimately approve the letter. Changes are simple to make and the outline classification will serve as an excellent prompt for your draft or dictation.

Using a sticky note for each heading and spreading these on your desk or a flipchart will allow you to change sequence without extensive crossing out or rewriting.

Form the paragraph structure

There are no rules for paragraphing that require us to break the text after a certain number of words or lines. Paragraphs have more to do with consistency of thought than with length. But there are guidelines that help convert planned content into readable paragraphs:

~ Change paragraph with each change of subject.

~ If your subject requires lengthy explanation, break it into further paragraphs that reflect the different aspects.

~ Headline your paragraph to give an early indication of your subject.

Many business letters deliver their thoughts on a single subject; a single paragraph will often serve. *

* A lengthy single paragraph filling most of an A4 page may look overpowering.

Many single page business letters appear in a three paragraph format that reflects:

~ identification

~ explanation

~ action.

In these cases the opening and closing paragraphs are often short – commonly a single sentence. The middle paragraph expands to the extent that is necessary to be complete.

Paragraph length is also a matter of writing style. Compare the paragraphs in the editorial section of a tabloid and a broadsheet newspaper and you will see how marked can be the contrast.

A single sentence can make an emphatic paragraph but over-use of single sentence paragraphs will diminish their effect.

Be wary when you edit your writing that you keep the integrity of your paragraph. *

If you divide a paragraph, see that you have a self-contained lead-in at the start of the new paragraph.

A common error is to leave an unattached pronoun that the reader will be obliged to attach:

The Works Committee will consider this at their next meeting.

Headline your new paragraph with a self-contained opening sentence:

The Works Committee will consider the supply of spare parts at their next meeting.

Control your sentence length

Writers struggling to construct a sentence are not so much concerned with which relative should introduce a relative clause or whether a pronoun has become too remote from its antecedent. They are concerned with finding the right words to convey their intended meaning to the reader.

Choose the lead-in

Avoid a long lead-in to sentences:

~ With regard to your previously stated request that ...

~ As already indicated it is permissible, but not mandatory, for those fulfilling the role of delegates to sub-committees, to ... *

Use your own words

If you find it difficult to express your thoughts just ask yourself: what am I really trying to say? The conversational answer that will come to mind should shine on paper albeit with a little editorial polish. You save yourself the effort of translating your thoughts into stilted business language; you save your reader from translating the stilted business language into the thought you had originally.

Check sentence length

Researchers have measured writing to see what makes it readable. Answers usually include the types of words used and the sentence length. Quoting an ideal sentence length will not allow for differences in reading ability but a target figure commonly suggested for a typical business reader is an average of twenty words per sentence.

* Place your subject at or near the start of the sentence.

Words are not just counted between full stops; the colon and the semi-colon also determine the sentence structure for this purpose.

Remember you are seeking a readable average sentence length; you are not trying to make every sentence twenty words long. Variety in sentence length will produce a more interesting style. Adding qualifying comment to a core sentence can test your skill. *

Adopt a conversational approach in your writing, control your sentence length and your relatives and antecedents should not trouble you.

Use a range of punctuation

The trend is to use only the punctuation you need to reveal your meaning. If you find yourself propping up a poor sentence with excessive punctuation, write it again.

Full stop

A sentence must contain a subject and a

*If the link between core components becomes too tenuous, rewrite the sentence or convert it into two.

finite verb; a finite verb is a verb that has been modified by its subject. A sentence must express a complete thought but can have a very simple structure:

John writes.
The sun is shining.

With reference to your letter of 14 March. is not a complete sentence despite the full stop.

Semicolon

The semicolon provides a useful pause lighter than a full stop but heavier than a comma. You will use it most reliably by ensuring that the elements you have linked could appear as independent sentences. *

Colon

Many writers in business use the colon to introduce a list.

During the move the following items were mislaid: a filing cabinet, a bunch of keys, a coat stand and several box files.

* The semicolon shows that the statements it joins are closely linked in sense; the link connects the ideas in the reader's mind.

The colon also allows you to define or illustrate an initial statement.

> After the war my circumstances had changed: I was disabled, unemployed and had little hope for the future.

Comma

There are many technical reasons for using commas but these are mainly to do with building a pause to indicate your meaning on first reading.

~ Use a comma when you wish to indicate such a pause.

~ Do not break a sentence, unnecessarily with a comma. (The comma in the previous sentence is unnecessary.)

~ Do not use a comma if you need a heavier stop, this applies even if the next point is linked. (A semicolon should replace the comma in the previous sentence.)

Brackets

Brackets enclose an aside or illustration and need no further punctuation. *

> Where the house is held on a tenancy in common by husband and wife it is possible (and useful for Capital Transfer Tax purposes) to avoid each half share going to the other spouse.

> The workshop covered more than 300 square metres (3230 square feet).

> (Previous attempts to recover this sum had produced similar results.)

Question marks

Use question marks only for direct questions.

> When will you send me the samples?

> The Senior Buyer asked if the samples would come fully assembled.

* They may enclose an entire sentence if it is commenting on a previous one.

Apostrophe

Rule 1

If you wish to show possession add an

apostrophe to the relevant word.

Rule 2
If it already ends in the letter s leave it; if it does not, add the letter s.

Tolerate the common exceptions with possessive pronouns:

> hers, yours, theirs, ours, its (but one's to distinguish from ones and twos). It's is a corruption of it is.

Try not to discover other exceptions that may challenge these workable rules. *

Summary Points

★ List your content.

★ Put it in sequence.

★ Develop paragraphs from the headings in your sequence.

★ Make sentences readable.

★ Use a range of punctuation to bring out your meaning.

* Your reader will not digest your writing if your punctuation sounds like hiccups.

3 Language and Style

Language is the dress of thought.

There is no single characteristic of style that you get either right or wrong in constructing your letter: many elements contribute to style. Some are structural and relate to paragraphs and sentences; others relate to your choice of words.

The English language derives from more than one source and contains a large vocabulary. You are not always seeking the single correct word but choosing from a number of possibilities. *

* *In avoiding repetition you may produce elegant variations that range more widely than is helpful for your reader.*

Writers and readers seek clarity and conciseness in letter writing. Familiar, concrete words delivered in the active voice will give you a good start. Avoiding clichés and controlling the technical content of writing will provide useful support in achieving an effective style.

Is this you?

I know what I want to say but I just can't find the words to say it. • I find official letters so hard to understand. • Will readers understand the technical detail? • I am expected to write in the passive voice. • What do they mean by "improving communications"? • I need to learn a few more standard business phrases.

Be active

Writers with a technical or scientific background may be inclined to write in the passive voice. For some the habit is a lesson learned from student days. "It is not up to you to say what you did but to show what was done." "People are not interested in you but in the research." The issue is partly in the use of the personal pronoun: the I or we that is everyday reference.

Many paragraphs begin in the third person passive voice:

~ It is suggested that . . .

~ It will be appreciated that . . .

~ It has been noted that . . .

It is true that the passive voice, by detaching the writer, can give writing more authority. But as an individual we are unlikely to say: "It is thought by me that the active voice is helpful for structuring letters." *

It is natural to say: "I have sent . . ." or "When can you deliver?"

It helps to know where a suggestion, decision or appreciation originates. In the passive voice the subject may remain without identification:

~ It was decided that . . .

~ The loan was refused . . .

In the active voice we identify our subject:

* *A business letter focuses on what you require of the reader or how you respond to the reader's need.*

~ The Bank Manager refused ...

~ The committee decided ...

~ The Senior Engineer authorised ...

In practice you will probably use both active and passive voices to reflect the emphasis you wish to place. You will find it natural to say: "The stationery was delivered this morning" as the concern is not with the person who delivered it but with the fact of its arrival. In the same breath and just as naturally you might add: "Sally signed for it." *

Choose familiar words

Formal styles are becoming more rare. Writers are more likely to thank you for your letter than to beg to acknowledge its receipt. You may still find it difficult to decide the degree of formality.

Be guided by the aim of the letter. An accountant writing to the Inland Revenue would adopt a formal style: he writes to an institution on a technical matter and not

* Write in the active voice for the natural directness that will result; the passive can be used to give a different slant to the reader.

normally to a named reader. The same accountant writing on a similar matter to an individual client is likely to adopt a more personal style.

Formality appears in words like:

advise, inform, notify, claim, state, learn, note, regret, trust.

Conversational English produces more familiar wording:

suggest, let you know, say, write, hear, understand, ask, hope.

Advocates of plain English argue for conversational style in all correspondence but to reflect differences of aim it is reasonable to present differences in style. Prefer less formal style when you can, particularly when you write to an individual. *

This will save you the mental anguish of searching for suitably formal language and will allow you to say what you mean.

You may feel uncomfortable when replying to a letter from a person unknown to you who has adopted an over-personal style. In such cases adopt the degree of formality that makes you feel comfortable.

Do not write "up" to your reader in the mistaken expectation that you will make a good impression:

~ Write send rather than transmit.

~ Write end rather than terminate.

~ But if you wish to convey the broader connotation of a word like remuneration, do not write pay.

The purpose is not to demonstrate your examination pass in English but to convey your intended meaning to the reader. Readers will not complain about finding your letter easy to understand.

You may sometimes find it difficult to think of any words at all. When this fate occasionally overtook a colleague, I would ask: "What are you trying to say?" *

The secret, of course, is to commit to paper the brief and lucid answer that naturally springs to mind.

Paint a concrete picture

Concrete nouns refer to tangible things the reader can visualise. Abstract nouns label ideas. You may need to float ideas but avoid dressing every concrete intention in a cloak of abstraction.

Compare the pictures that result:

~ 5% rate of interest
  - moderate growth of assets

~ letter of 16 December
  - communication of recent date

~ 40 tonne container lorry
  - bulk transportation

If a writer exhorted you to use the services of his business to improve company communications would you expect to buy a new computer system or sign up to a lease purchase agreement for the firm's fleet of cars?

Some writers try to impress their readers by adopting an erudite vocabulary. The impression they create may not be quite the one they intended. Reassure yourself that the concrete approach is right by imagining that you are the reader of the letter rather than the writer.

The process begins at school when your teacher says:" You have used this word already in your essay. Try to think of something else." The teacher is right to develop your vocabulary. *

Familiar concrete words show a clear profile. Superfluous or abstract words act only as camouflage.

It would be reasonable to exclude diplomacy from guidelines on abstract English. Abstraction softens the hard edges of the concrete and you are more likely to read: we have reservations about the suitability of your proposed course of action than: we don't like your idea.

Avoid clichés

Clichés are words, phrases and clauses that express an idea particularly well and gradually fall into regular use. They tempt the writer by their familiar convenience. The problem is in regular repetition that suggests the words are determined routinely with

* *It is that developed vocabulary that allows you to be selective in painting a forceful picture.*

little thought for the reader.

Clichés are most prevalent where writers find it hard to express themselves, such as at the beginning or end of a letter. Does their difficulty result from the abundance of clichés?

The beginning of a letter identifies your reason for writing. You may need to acknowledge or refer, to thank or request. You do this best in your own words. *

In the explanatory part of the letter wordy phrases can take over:

Due to the fact that ...
In the event that ...
With regard to ...

A single preposition will replace these:

... because ...
If ...
... about ...

*Prune flowery language and in some cases, uproot it:

* Prefer to thank someone for their letter of a particular date rather than to acknowledge receipt of recent correspondence.

It will be appreciated that ...
It is suggested that ...
May we take this opportunity to ...

Time references account for many clichés:
in due course
in the not too distant future
at your earliest convenience.

Try putting those in order of urgency. The Victorian clerk may be praised for penning that perfect balance of courtesy and urgency:
as soon as possible

but millions of daily readers would see in that expression little incentive to respond. *

The end of a letter should point to the next action. Leave your reader quite clear as to what you expect. When you have finished what you wish to say, sign off: Yours faithfully, Yours sincerely. Avoid the empty gesture of a concluding paragraph:

Assuring you of our best attention at all times.

* *Its meaning has been lost in the frequency of its repetition.*

(You assure the reader by the manner in which you deal with his letter.)

Looking forward to your early reply.

(If your letter depends on this final request, it has failed to meet its aim.)

If I can be of any further assistance please do not hesitate to contact me.

(The excessive use of this expression has left it with little meaning.) If you really intend the reader to come back to you, make it sound as if you mean it:

If you need more information, please telephone me on extension 491.

Underlying many of these concluding clichés is the feeling that you need to be courteous as you may have put the reader to some trouble. *

* Courtesy should be in the way you deal with an issue, not in the cliché at the end.

When you don't know how to end your letter, you have probably ended it already. That is the point at which you should sign off.

Control jargon and technical language

A systems analyst, a solicitor, a butter maker, a personnel officer, a capstan lathe operator, a book-keeper will use terms unfamiliar to those outside their field. The technical language relates to the techniques each uses and will have a standard meaning for anyone doing similar work. In a letter, a materials scientist would expect to write about composites just as you would expect your greengrocer to talk about potatoes.

You can deliver technical language at different levels.

To the informed specialist:

~ Our research indicated that pre-flooding produced stirring of the packed bed ...

To the uninformed we may have more impact by saying:

~ Our research has shown that if the flow of water through the filter is too great, you will disturb the material in the filter and make it less effective.

The non-technical explanation may need more words.

Where the need is less clear you can emphasize the technical (by removing any definition or explanation to a bracket):

~ Our research indicated that pre-flooding (a high liquid flow rate) produced stirring (derangement) of the packed bed ...

You can emphasize the general (by bracketing the technical term):

~ Our research indicated that a high liquid flow rate (pre-flooding) produced derangement of the packed bed (stirring) ...

Jargon can be more challenging. It may deliver a technical content but it can be very local in its use. It may describe a document, a product or manufacturing process, a system, a service. *

* *You will find it hard to escape the use of jargon.*

Jargon is most dangerous when it assumes the form of a familiar word. You may think of a barrel as the container in which the little pig rolled down the hill. To a brewer a barrel is a precise measure of beer; to an oilman it is an equally precise, but different, measure of oil.

Jargon can appear as an abbreviation and your explanation can come in the form of expansion to the original. You may need to refer to damp proof course (dpc) before leaving your reader with the solitary reference: dpc.

Numbers are a common jargon reference. We may be asked to complete a GW 240 for which the only identification is a minute reference at the foot of the document. Many people would know a P45; few could quote the words that describe it.

There are times when we should not tolerate jargon. The water company official who wrote to a consumer: "The peak often reaches 150% of demand" should have been turned off like the water he was trying to save. *

More explanatory language should serve.

But it can be good communication to use the client's jargon. Every accountant in the land would describe a certain record as the purchase ledger. If that is known to your client as the blue book you must be guided by that expectation.

Jargon can be bizarre. When working with a transport organisation I heard a bus driver commenting on the large number of "twirlies" who were in the habit of boarding his bus. I discovered later that the reference was to pensioners with bus passes. The pass comes into force after the morning rush and the inevitable question at about that time was: "Good morning. Am I too early?"

Summary Points

★ Write in the active voice.

★ Use familiar words.

★ Paint a clear, concrete picture.

★ Avoid clichés.

★ Keep control of jargon and technical language.

4 Layout of Your Letter

Frame the picture.

Y ou may wonder why we retain conventions such as the salutation at the start of a letter and the complimentary close at the end. We begin Dear Mr Brown and then we tear him apart for some major failure. The last true feeling about the reader is that he is in any way dear to us. *

Letters have become less formal and word processing gives many more options for the alignment and appearance of text than a layout that was once dictated by the mechanical limitations of the typewriter. The majority of letters are left aligned only, leaving a ragged right margin that appears less formal and aids reading. Key information such as the reference, date, address,

* But it is the conventions that give the letter its form and distinguish it from memorandum, fax and e-mail.

salutation, complimentary close and enclosures is increasingly aligned to the left margin.

Letterheads have changed too. Once all information appeared at the top of the page. Now you may see the company logo prominent at the top but much of the statutory detail at the foot. *

Consider how your letter will appear when it reaches your reader. If you have folded it twice with several enclosures to fit a standard window envelope it may look less impressive than when you completed the admired layout by adding your most careful signature.

Is this you?

How should I start my letter? • Should I list enclosures on the letter or just on the copy? • Should I write Dear Sir or Dear Sirs? • What should I put at the end? • Do I need a heading? • How do I sign off if I am writing the letter for someone else?

* This is tidier but leaves less room for the script.

Quote references in full

We put a reference on a letter so that when someone replies quoting the reference, we are able easily to find the letter on file. Always quote a reference when replying. Much correspondence is stored electronically and the quoted reference may be the only manageable way of retrieving a particular letter. *

One common layout will begin:

    Reference
    Date
    Address of reader
    ....
    ....
    ....

An alternative layout (perhaps a little more traditional) will show:

Address of reader	Your ref:
....	Our ref:
....	Date:
....	

If there is no reference, identify the letter to which you reply by quoting the subject and date.

In the second example, the prompts Your ref: Our ref: Date: will often appear in print on the letterhead and their position will reflect the letter template on the word processor. When you initiate correspondence the section Your ref: remains empty. *

Look to the address not simply to direct your letter to the receiving organisation but to the individual from whom you seek a response. It is now usual practice to include the name and job title of the recipient as part of the address. As that information appears through the window in the envelope, your letter can be targeted unopened to its reader.

Choose an apt salutation

Try to include the name in the salutation at the start of your letter. This will help to:

~ get commitment from a reader whom you have targeted precisely

~ set a personal tone for your writing.

One benefit of this more traditional layout is that you use less of the page for the reference information.

Writers sometimes identify themselves just with name and initials at the end of their letter. You will see Yours sincerely ... J R Hartley. We have a practical problem in that we need to attach a style (Mr Mrs Miss Ms) to the reply. Those who are not too concerned with gender may still feel displeased at being identified as Mr if they are Ms or Ms if they are Mr. Control rests with the writer who may wish to add the style at the close of the letter:

   Yours sincerely   (Mrs) J R Hartley

For some the name is critical to an effective reply. A salesman replying to an enquiry would wish to build the benefits of his product or service for a named reader. He may even telephone to establish the style of his reader and if a first name emerges it may appear as part of the reply address:

   Miss Chloe Thompson
   Glasshouse Manufacturing
   Basingstoke ...

   Dear Miss Thompson

The first name is helpful in making the personal link in the address, but Dear Chloe would be presumptuous as a salutation at this early stage of contact.

Very formal style still appears in business letters. You may occasionally find a letter that begins:

> For the attention of Mr R T Jones
>
> Dear Sirs
> We acknowledge the telephone conversation of 13th March between your Mr Jones and the writer and your request ... *

A name allows you to be more natural and direct:

> Dear Mr Jones
>
> When we spoke on the telephone today, you asked ...

* Such style does little for public relations or for your composing.

You will need a formal salutation when you write to an institution rather than a named reader:

Dear Sir   Dear Sirs   Dear Madam

A PLC or a Limited Company is a single legal entity and it is logical to address the company as Dear Sir. Nonetheless you will see many letters addressed to John Smith Limited that begin Dear Sirs. The assumption of the writer may be that he writes to the board of directors or members of the company rather than the company as an entity. Certainly the form Dear Sirs is correct when we write to a partnership where partners have "joint and several liability".

Avoid writing Dear Sir/Madam. Whichever part of that generalisation you attach to, it is offensive for its failure to relate properly to you. *

A local authority can address a diversity of readers as:

Dear Tenant
Dear Occupier
Dear Householder

* *A general name can make a good alternative.*

Similarly, your letter to an unnamed Inspector of Taxes may begin:

Dear Inspector

Use informative headings

Most letters benefit from a heading. This serves to:

~ tell the reader what you are writing about

~ provide a descriptive reminder of the content of a letter you may later wish to retrieve. *

In an extensive letter distinguish between a heading that covers the broad scope of the letter at the start:

Firtree Farm Contract
Annual Audit J Davis
Training Programme

and the more specific headings that occur at intervals to identify the specific topics of the letter.

* *Make headings concrete so you paint a clear picture.*

In a short letter you may write predominantly on one topic but then wish to make a small unrelated point later. This need produces clichés like:

May I take this opportunity to remind ...

While you are right to take the opportunity you will make a clear case by putting your thought under a separate heading. The letter will take on the form:

Salutation
Heading One
....
....
....
Heading Two
....
Close

Think about the sequence in which you handle your headings. Where possible end with the topic that needs action.

Bullet points form a practical sub-structure for letters. They are best for items that require separate identification but which need no specific reference.

Before I can agree to an overdraft I will
need:
- your monthly income
- your monthly outgoings
- the amount of any other loans
- hire purchase debt.

A sub-structure of numbers is helpful where
you wish to raise a number of points which
require a specific answer from your reader. *

Start with your reason for writing

Use the start of your letter to identify your
reason for writing. When you initiate
correspondence, spell out your intention for
the reader. A heading will provide the initial
view but your opening sentence will sharpen
the focus:

~ I am writing for information about your
counselling service.

~ I am planning a short visit to Rome in
March . . .

*Using the number
as a reference for
the reply is
informative to the
originator.*

~ When I met your Technical Director at the
   National Packaging Exhibition last week ...

When responding to a letter you have a
similar need to provide a clear focus for the
reader. You may wish to use the heading
from the original letter before responding
more specifically:

~ Thank you for your letter of 12 November.

~ I confirm that we manufacture tubular
   steel furniture that would be suitable for
   use in your canteen.

~ The timetable with this letter should give
   you all the information you need to plan
   your journey.

Avoid the tempting clichés:

   We (beg to) acknowledge receipt of
   your letter of 11th July.

   Further to your letter of 17 June ...

Some very short letters end where they
begin:

~ Please send me two copies of your current stationery catalogue and price list.

~ I confirm that I will attend the meeting at Scott House on 4 July and plan to arrive in good time for the start at 10 am. *

End by pointing the way ahead

The end of your letter is important in triggering the action you seek from the reader:

~ Please let me know when you will be able to deliver the materials.

~ Please send the completed application form with your cheque by 20 June.

The true aim of the letter may vary from the issue that has prompted it. In such cases project your purpose at the end. Imagine you have to send a client an invoice for completed work. A covering letter can end by showing your continuing interest:

~ We would be very pleased to undertake

There is no point in extending this complete information into a more complex format.

further work for you next year.

~ I will contact you again in November to see if you wish to advertise in the spring edition.

Long letters containing a number of action points may benefit from a short summary of actions at the end.

Avoid clichés at the end of your letter. These usually appear when you have covered the ground and are ready to sign off. Padding at this point pushes the required action further back into the letter, making it less of a prompt for the reader's attention. *

Match the close to the salutation

The convention for matching the close to the salutation is firm:

If you begin with a proper noun:

Dear Mr Brown   Dear Ms Patel
Dear Mrs Jones   Dear James
Dear Miss Smith   Dear Sophie

* *It can be right to end by inviting someone to contact you for further detail if by doing so you further the aim of the letter.*

you end:

Yours sincerely

Similarly if you begin with a common noun:

Dear Tenant
Dear Householder
Dear Inspector

you end:

Yours sincerely

(Use the capital letter for the common noun because you are relating it to a specific individual.)

For formal salutations:
Dear Sir
Dear Madam
Dear Sirs

you end:

Yours faithfully

Other forms are rare and any attempt to

combine salutation and close differently would be described by many as "wrong".

To give a more personal touch to correspondence (even widely circulated standard letters) some writers like to write by hand the salutation and the close. This allows them to add a personal comment that is "off the record" *

There are many reasons why the signatory of the letter may not be the correspondent whose name appears in print. Usually the printed name is the person authorised to act. J Smith may sign for B Brown, Borough Engineer where B Brown is the senior person in the department and J Smith the person dealing with the particular issue.

The signature may appear as J Smith pp B Brown where pp abbreviates the Latin per et pro, normally translated as 'for and on behalf of'. The preposition 'for' will serve as well.

It is more difficult to pretend to be someone

* Remember that while the personal comment is off your record it is on the record at the receiving end.

else when writing a letter. You may experience some discomfort in writing:

> I will ask my colleague John Smith to contact you next week ...

when you are indeed the John Smith who will make contact. It is clearly more satisfactory to write as yourself and to target a named reader but the formality of the system in your organisation may force you to respond at times in that way.

Always sign off in a way that gives a clear identification for the reader's reply. Your name and a job title or department name would inform:

Tom Jones	Bertrand Russell
Sales Administrator	Accounts *

Summary Points

★ Quote your reader's reference.

★ Choose a relevant salutation and link it to the close.

* Start as you intend to finish.

★ Write informative headings.

★ Start by telling the reader why you are
   writing.

★ Be sure the action you need is clear at the
   end.

5 Strategies for Business Letters

Plan to succeed.

Writing an effective letter is not just about putting information on paper. You will sometimes need to present a well-argued case. As well as reader and content you will need to consider:

~ the sequence in which you deliver your case, and

~ the tone reflected in your choice of words.

A harsh tone may allow you to reprimand a wayward supplier but would it be apt for your long-standing client – even if you are temporarily displeased?

Look at your incoming mail. See what gets your attention in an unsolicited letter and encourages you to read on. If you were not encouraged to read on, check why. Did the letter make clear what was expected of you? If not, why did it fail? Use the constructive features of other people's letters to develop your own style.

Is this you?

How firm should I be? • Do I apologise for the mistake? • Should I ask at the beginning or at the end? • Should I send a letter as well as a brochure? • Do I include a quotation? • Why did they not act on my last letter?

Sequence your letter to achieve your aim

The sequence of a letter allows you to move:

~ from where you are now

~ by means of supporting information

~ to where you wish to be. *

The sequence is more a progression than a chronology in many cases.

Reviewing performance

~ Outline where the business has come from.

~ Show where it is now.

~ Describe what we plan for the future.

Proposing agenda for an annual conference

~ Review the issues arising from last year.

~ List current concerns within the business.

~ Define issues that will arise in the ensuing year.

Following death of a member of staff

~ Express shock at sad news.

~ Show appreciation of the person and their work.

~ Offer support to bereaved person.

For simplicity these sequences show a beginning, a middle, and an end. But there may be many stages between the starting point and the point where you feel the information is complete. Taking trouble with your sequence will:

~ prompt your writing to flow easily

~ help your reader to follow your argument

~ give your letter the authority of a well-reasoned case. *

Choose an appropriate tone

When you write, your words convey both the content of your writing and the manner of its delivery. Tone is very evident. Clearly you will want this transparency to work to your advantage.

Expressing regret

It is with deep regret that we learn of your dissatisfaction with ...

sounds pompous and unconvincing.

I was sorry to hear of your difficulty in boarding the bus ...

* *Order your thoughts to end in achievement.*

expresses a genuine concern for the reader's welfare.

Handling a complaint

Using words like inconvenience, dissatisfaction or even complaint provides a negative reminder of the problem that triggered the correspondence. You acknowledge inconvenience or dissatisfaction by dealing positively with the reply.

Taking to task

One connotation of words like You claimed ... or You stated ... is that you do not entirely believe what is claimed or is stated. That may be your occasional intention but you would perhaps achieve more by saying: You wished to ... You said ... You wrote about ...

Seeking action

By now you will recognise that as soon as possible is no more than a vague hope for the future. To ask for something now or yesterday may work when you are able to inflect suitable humour on the telephone but will be abrupt or challenging on paper. A date by which you need something may be a reasonable target for the reader's action, particularly when you point out how helpful its achievement would be.

Aim for the simple, natural vocabulary you would use if you were to give your explanation face to face. If you have overcome your reader's problem, end positively. Many a good letter has failed by ending: Once again we apologise for any inconvenience caused. *

Give or get information clearly

Much regular business correspondence involves an exchange of information. The theme of enquiries will illustrate some of the needs.

* Optimism generates a positive response where pessimism gets filed at the bottom of the in-tray.

Making an enquiry

Try to target the right reader but if you cannot be certain who this is, add a defining heading to your letter. Make your need clear.

Present a specification as a bullet list; aim to be complete. Offer a telephone number (especially a direct dial or extension number) so that you may clarify points of detail.

It is hard to be complete when specifying a requirement. After presenting an extensive list you may still be asked if you want the flat ends or the round ends, or if you would like the casing in grey or black.

Answering an enquiry

Provide the information that is asked for, plainly. Give additional information only when you consider it relevant to the original enquiry. But you may add a persuasive slant. After all there is little point in manufacturing widgets if you can't sell them.

If the enquiry is outside your field say so, and, if possible, say who may be able to help. This will not cost you business but will gain goodwill. *

* If you also say what you can do, you may create an opportunity to sell in the future.

Following up an enquiry

If your first response to an enquiry fails to produce business, don't despair. Follow up with additional information about your product or service. Point to a possible visit to discuss the need in more detail. If you follow up after the visit, use the letter to consolidate the goodwill generated by the personal contact.

Acknowledging an order

Don't give up your effort when you receive the order: only now does your customer feel committed to your organisation. You may need to get additional information about the address for delivery or the method of payment. You may also give additional information about what will happen next or indicating other relevant products or services. Someone who has bought a few rolls of wallpaper may be in the market for a bucket, some paste and a brush.

Handle complaints with tact and authority

When you reply to a complaint you have an excellent opportunity to build goodwill.

Always show understanding; don't let a grudging reluctance show in your reply. A sound strategy for handling a complaint will again be about:

~ the sequence in which you deliver the information

~ the tone of your reply.

When you are at fault

~ Thank them for their letter.

~ Apologise for the problem.

~ Explain what caused it or what you are doing to investigate the cause.

~ Say what you have done or will do to put it right.

and sometimes:

~ Say how they might avoid the problem in future.

The reader will not be concerned with your problems but by saying what went wrong you are able to show that there was a good reason and that you are not indifferent to the issue. Ideally this type of letter will end by saying what you have done to put the matter right. When this is not possible "how to prevent in future" can be a reasonable alternative.

When you wish to make a concesssion

~ Thank them for their letter.

~ Express sympathy ... sorry to hear that ...

~ Say what you will do about it.

~ Say how they can prevent this happening another time.

This type of letter is very common in business. It applies when we are not at fault but when, in the interests of goodwill, we wish to respond to a customer's complaint. *

When you wish to stand firm

~ Thank them for their letter.

~ Show some sympathy.

The "how to prevent in future" can give a tactful reminder that you may not be quite so generous in making a concession another time.

~ Show that you understand the point they are making.

then:

~ Give your own point of view.

~ Continue by saying that you cannot therefore respond as they wish.

~ Conclude by pointing out how they can avoid the problem another time.

This letter provides a Yes ... but answer. We hear what you say but we are not willing to concede. By showing that you have understood the basis of their complaint your negative response has authority.

With all letters of complaint, end on the positive note you have planned. *

Readers of this section may be concerned, particularly in these days of increasing litigation, about admitting liability in a letter when replying to a complaint. Matters of such concern will require the response of a lawyer rather than a writer of routine letters.

Don't spoil the finish by apologising again or by reminding them of their concern.

But there are many everyday needs for apology:

~ incorrectly completed form

~ late delivery

~ overlooked document

~ missed appointment.

where a well-written reply will build goodwill.

Get timely action

When you write asking for action you cannot guarantee that action will follow. But you can make action more likely if you:

~ give the reader an incentive to act

~ make clear precisely what you need

~ place the request to act at the point where it is most likely to prompt the action.

Our interest is to outline the problem, making clear what we need and when we need it. We encourage the reader by showing understanding of the effect of our request and giving some incentive to respond. Put together these components and you have useful elements for a letter seeking action:

~ Identify the issue.

~ Show you understand how this affects the reader.

~ Point out what you need from the reader.

~ Give some incentive to act.

~ Say when the action should happen.

Leave the request for action to the end of the letter. *

Give a specific date for reply if you need to. Don't hide behind a modest courtesy by saying:

> Perhaps you will be good enough to let me know if . . .

or:

* If action is in the form of an answer, prompt it by a direct question and make sure you include the question mark.

I would appreciate an early indication of ...

A date for action can help the reader to plan the response and should not sound unreasonably demanding if you have taken trouble with the tone of your letter.

When your letter has more than one function, sequence it so that the action you seek comes at the end. Eliminate earlier, reasons that might otherwise prevent the action from happening.

The letter that follows is a reply to a complaint but the writer also seeks an outstanding payment:

Dear Mr Jones

Thank you for your letter of 30 March. I am sorry that we overcharged you (as you correctly pointed out) for two quarterly standing charges.

I have credited your account with £40.80 to cover the overcharge and this makes the amount now due for settlement £109.48.

Yours sincerely

John Smith
Accounts Department *

Promote your product or service

Computers generate enormous numbers of
selling letters. For a selling letter to make an
impact it will need originality. It will also
need a progressive framework to prompt the
reader's response:

~ Capture the reader's interest.

~ Point out the benefits of your product or
  service.

~ Anticipate objections and overcome them.

~ Persuade the customer to act.

Capture the reader's interest

** Suit the action to
the word, the
word to the action*

Use humour, an anecdote, a quotation, or an
appeal to get the initial interest of your
reader. Identify a matter of current interest if

you can. Local newspapers are a good
source of relevant ideas from key staff
appointments to who is planning a new
building.

Point out the benefits of your product or service

Brochures and catalogues tend to feature
items in a general way that is not always
appropriate for the customer you may have
in mind. Translate "features" into "benefits"
for your particular customer. If you are
selling chairs with a siliconised finish, tell
your customer the chairs can stay out on the
terrace in all weathers without deteriorating.
If you lead a team of 30 service engineers,
tell the customer you can have an engineer
to their home or office the following day.
The feature of having 30 service engineers
translates into the benefit to the customer of
rapid service.

Anticipate objections and overcome them

However good your product or service there

could be characteristics to which a potential customer might object: the price, the time until delivery, the limited choice of colour ...

Anticipate the more obvious objections and counter them with relevant benefits.

Although the quality of this product makes it a little more expensive you will soon be repaid by regular time saving in daily use and by the need for little maintenance. Follow-up letters may need to handle objections raised by the customer.

Persuade the customer to act

Seek a positive response or point of agreement even if this is on a relatively minor matter. Leave opportunities for follow-up: I will telephone you next week to see if you would like our representative to call. A direct question can be a good prompt for a reply. *

* Everyone lives by selling something.

Summary Points

★ Sequence your letter to end as you intend.

★ Match the tone to the reader's need.

★ Give and get information clearly.

★ Use complaints to build goodwill.

★ Prompt timely action at the end.

★ Sell by turning features into benefits.

6 Editing and Proofreading

Give us the tools and we will finish the job.

An effective editor needs a range of skills. Sound knowledge of modern English usage must complement understanding of the conventions on capital letters, abbreviations and the use of numbers. The letter must look right on the page but also be correct in the detail of spelling and punctuation. Few people aspire to that expertise but we can all seek a good appearance for our letter and expect to deliver a clear message relatively free from errors of spelling and grammar.

Allow time for proofreading; see the task as part of the writing process. *

* Try to leave an interval between writing and editing so that the letter is fresh and you may be more objective in your review.

Take regular breaks: concentration can be short-lived and enthusiasm can wane.

You may wish to use an independent reader especially if you are trying to compare the dead copy (original draft) with the live copy, the typed version. Effort now will give impact to the final version.

Is this you?

Should I use capital letters for buying officer?
• Do I need punctuation with bullet points?
• If I proofread it now it will miss the post •
Can I start a sentence with but? • Can I send out my letter with a handwritten correction?
• I keep missing errors on the screen.

Focus your proofreading

Many working environments are not ideal for proofreading so try to find space where you can work comfortably without interruption. Have everything you need ready.

The dead copy, that is the original draft or manuscript, will also need to relate to the live copy, that is the screen or typescript you are proofreading. If you are working directly from the screen without a draft you may prefer to proofread from a printed copy.*

If your letter is complex or technical you may prefer to enrol help to read the dead copy while you concentrate on the live copy.

Proofreading is about detail but we need to be aware of the broader impression of the piece of writing. Proofread for:

~ visual impression

~ sense of the message

~ accuracy of the detail.

Visual impression

What does the page look like? Is there too much detail? Is there enough white space? Is the page balanced between top and bottom? If there is a large gap at the bottom, is this intended?

Is the text justified? Is it aligned to the left only?

Are headings too large or too small?

Is the size of typeface appropriate?

* Many people miss errors on the screen, particularly where the word processor does not allow a full view of the line in one fix.

Reading for sense

This can severely test our knowledge of grammar and our ability to write clearly.

Are the paragraph breaks in the right places? Are sentences too long? Even if the average length is right, is there enough variety in sentence structure?

Are there errors of grammar? Is the word order correct? Is the message clear? Is the vocabulary apt for the reader?

Reading for detail

Is the punctuation in the right place?
Is the correct punctuation mark in place?
Is the spelling correct?
Are there typographical errors? *

Know where to find errors

* This section contains many questions. They will remind you to test at several levels before accepting that text is correct.

You are less likely to miss an error if you know where errors are likely to be. Expect to find errors:

~ at the start of text

~ near other errors

~ in common words: not/now there/the
   and/an

~ repeating from the end of a line to the
   beginning of the next line

~ in changes from standard type

~ in changes of page formation: margins,
   columns.

It is easy to rationalise these errors. Changes
of type or page formation cause us to think
about control instructions rather than the
flow of typing. Some word processing
software will not show the end of one line
and the beginning of the next line
simultaneously on the monitor. Instinct may
take over from reason with regularly typed
common words. Awareness of a possible
error may distract sufficiently to cause
another. False starts are routine in many
daily activities. *

*Keep control by
knowing where to
look.*

You will be reassured by the relative ease
with which you will find errors such as
omitted letters, spaces, punctuation marks or

substitutions of one letter for another. You will also be aware of the need for relentless concentration to do so.

Check you are clear and concise

No single aspect of your writing will produce a clear, concise style: you will need to review a number of elements.

Sequence

~ Check that your letter achieves a progression of ideas.

~ See that you move from where you are at the start to where you wish to be at the end.

Paragraphs

A paragraph that might suit an extensive report can look excessive when filling the space under a letterhead.

~ Make paragraphs in letters relatively short.

~ Make the topic of each paragraph clear.

~ If you have divided a paragraph, see that
the new paragraph has a clear headline
and is not left dangling by a pronoun.

Sentences

~ Check your sentence length.

~ Aim for an average of 20 words but vary
sentence length for interest.

~ Remember that a series of short sentences
can read like a menu.

Punctuation

~ See that punctuation properly supports
the structure of your writing.

~ Be sure the reader will absorb your
meaning on a single reading.

~ If the punctuation is struggling to reveal
your meaning, rewrite the sentence.

Active voice

~ Link subject and verb directly by
presenting your case in the active voice.

~ Avoid long passive leads-in:

It will be appreciated that ...
It is suggested that ...
It has been noted that ...

Familiar words

~ Use familiar words that will be
  comfortable for the reader. *

Concrete words

~ Use concrete words to paint a clear picture
  for the reader.

~ Make your specification explicit and
  complete.

Clichés

~ Avoid over-used business expressions.

~ Use your own words to set the right tone
  and help a flow of ideas.

Jargon

~ Use jargon to tune in to the reader.

** Avoid business
language.*

~ Avoid jargon that will sound out of tune.

Fulfil your aim

The most fluent and clear of letters will be unhelpful if they fail to fulfil their aim. *

Ask yourself key questions:

~ Who will read my letter?

~ What does my reader need to know?

~ What did I need to know?

~ Is the required action clear?

~ Will the reader know when to respond?

Satisfy yourself that you have fulfilled your aim and you will satisfy your reader.

Summary Points

★ Allow time for proofreading.

★ Try to work without distraction.

★ Look at the broad view as well as the detail.

★ Know where to expect errors.

* *In reviewing your draft you have the opportunity to come full circle and confirm that your letter does indeed fulfil its aim.*

★ Check that your message is clear.

★ Be sure you have achieved you aim.